S0-AVO-569

WITHDRAWN

ALTERNATOR
BOOKS™

WHO INVENTED THE
AIRPLANE?

WRIGHT BROTHERS VS. WHITEHEAD

Karen Latchana Kenney

Lerner Publications ◆ Minneapolis

Copyright © 2018 by Lerner Publishing Group, Inc.

All rights reserved. International copyright secured. No part of this book may be reproduced, stored in a retrieval system, or transmitted in any form or by any means—electronic, mechanical, photocopying, recording, or otherwise—without the prior written permission of Lerner Publishing Group, Inc., except for the inclusion of brief quotations in an acknowledged review.

Lerner Publications Company
A division of Lerner Publishing Group, Inc.
241 First Avenue North
Minneapolis, MN 55401 USA

For reading levels and more information, look up this title at www.lernerbooks.com.

Library of Congress Cataloging-in-Publication Data

Names: Kenney, Karen Latchana, author.
Title: Who invented the airplane? : Wright Brothers vs. Whitehead / Karen Latchana Kenney.
Description: Minneapolis : Lerner Publications, [2018] | Series: STEM smackdown | Audience: Age 8–12. | Audience: Grade 4 to 6. | Includes bibliographical references and index.
Identifiers: LCCN 2017022030 (print) | LCCN 2017027793 (ebook) | ISBN 9781512483253 (eb pdf) | ISBN 9781512483185 (lb : alk. paper) | ISBN 9781541512061 (pb : alk. paper)
Subjects: LCSH: Whitehead, Gustave, 1874–1927. | Wright, Wilbur, 1867–1912. | Wright, Orville, 1871–1948. | Aeronautics—Juvenile literature. | Aeronautics—History—Juvenile literature.
Classification: LCC TL547 (ebook) | LCC TL547 .K3945 2018 (print) | DDC 629.130092/2—dc23

LC record available at https://lccn.loc.gov/2017022030

Manufactured in the United States of America
1-43331-33151-9/7/2017

CONTENTS

INTRODUCTION
THE AERONAUTS

Sitting in your airplane seat, you can't stop smiling. The airplane speeds down the runway and lifts. It climbs higher. Soon you're cruising at 35,000 feet (10,670 m). It's time to recline and watch a movie on your personal screen. Just think—in a few hours, you'll be in Hawaii!

Traveling by airplane is how most of us get to faraway places. But in the early twentieth century, flight was still a dream. Many tried to get into the air—and many failed. Inventors like Octave Chanute and Otto Lilienthal created **gliders** in the nineteenth century. They were the first aeronauts, a new group of people who had traveled by air. Some gliders lifted people into the sky and traveled a short distance.

To many people these days, flying seems like no big deal. But in the Wright brothers' time, it seemed extraordinary!

This drawing shows an early aircraft created by Otto Lilienthal.

But controlled, powered flight eluded even the best glider makers. Was it possible?

Many inventors gave up on conquering the skies, but some persisted. The biggest names in the competition were the Wright brothers, two bicycle mechanics from Ohio. Another contender was German immigrant Gustave Whitehead, a former sailor, mechanic, and coal miner. These aeronauts raced to be the first in flight. Who would soar across the finish line first? And who would be able to prove it?

CHAPTER 1

CHAMPS OF FLIGHT

If it was mechanical, the young Wright brothers from Dayton, Ohio, were interested in it. Toy flying machines, **gyroscopes**, and even sewing machines fascinated them. Born in 1867, Wilbur Wright was smart and careful. His brother Orville, born four years later, was a risk-taker. He seemed to be a natural-born inventor, taking things apart to see how they worked. The combination of their personalities led to a perfect partnership—one that led them into business together.

Gyroscopes, like this toy from the mid-twentieth century, fascinated the Wright brothers when they were growing up.

Orville Wright (*left*) and Wilbur Wright (*right*) were creative and curious from the very start!

They started a printing press and then moved to bicycles, opening the Wright Cycle Company. By about 1896, the brothers had a new interest—gliding. They read about Lilienthal's experiments and learned of his fatal crash in 1896. Wilbur wondered whether they could pick up where Lilienthal left off.

ENTERING THE RING

In 1899 the brothers researched gliding experiments. This was the beginning of their training. They began thinking of ways to solve the problems that had taken others out of the competition.

Two big problems were control and balance. To turn a glider, its wings had to be unbalanced. One side needed to be higher than the other. How could a glider stay balanced when its wings weren't? The answer came from a bicycle inner tube box in 1899. Wilbur twisted the box and saw that one corner went up while the opposite corner went down. It led to the brothers' wing warping idea. They built a kite with a device to warp the wings.

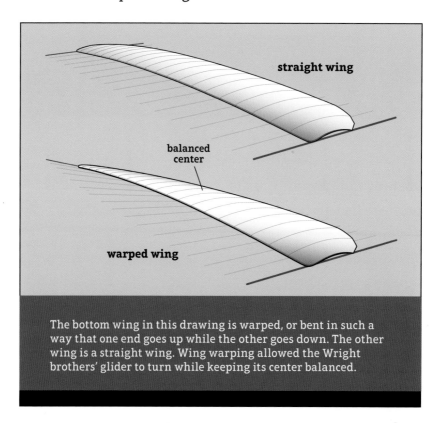

The bottom wing in this drawing is warped, or bent in such a way that one end goes up while the other goes down. The other wing is a straight wing. Wing warping allowed the Wright brothers' glider to turn while keeping its center balanced.

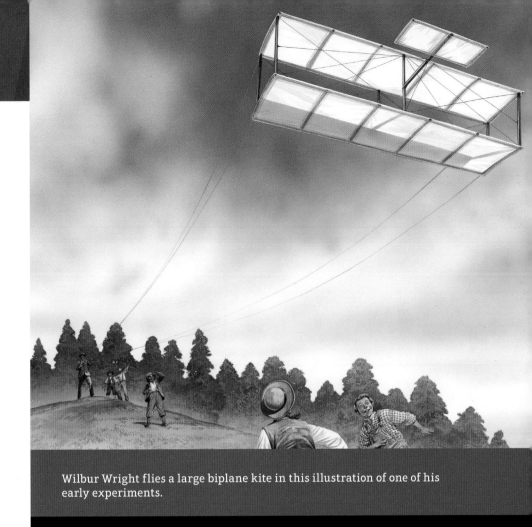

Wilbur Wright flies a large biplane kite in this illustration of one of his early experiments.

TESTS

The Wrights tested their kite and saw that wing warping worked. The kite turned left and right. Then they built a glider that could carry a person and found the right place to test it—Kitty Hawk, North Carolina. It was windy there, especially in September. They approached these trials scientifically, recording data and taking photographs.

Their first tests happened in 1900 at Kitty Hawk and then nearby Kill Devil Hills. The brothers watched for problems and took the data back to Ohio. They refined their designs, changing wing shapes to improve **lift**. They added **rudders** to increase stability. They returned to Kill Devil Hills in 1901 and 1902. After some failures in 1901, they came up with a much more successful design.

THEY DID WHAT?

The Wrights' 1901 tests were disappointing. The bigger glider they made didn't fly as well as the 1900 glider. They seemed to be going backward. Wilbur Wright later wrote about how they felt after the tests: "We doubted that we would ever resume our experiments. . . . At this time I made the prediction that men would sometime fly, but that it would not be within our lifetime."

The Wright brothers sometimes got discouraged but kept going even when faced with obstacles.

The Wright brothers' December 1903 flight was a success! Here Orville Wright lies on the flier's lower wing with his hips in the cradle that controlled the wing-warping device. His brother Wilbur looks on from the ground.

The inventors returned again in 1903. This time, their glider had a motor and **propellers**—it was a flier! On December 17, Orville Wright sat at the controls as the flier took off. It flew about 100 feet (30 m). Witness John T. Daniels snapped a picture. Four other witnesses watched in amazement. They'd just seen powered flight. To them it was a knockout win, but had someone beaten them to the punch?

CHAPTER 2

A SERIOUS CONTENDER

The Wrights weren't the only ones experimenting with flight. Gustave Whitehead was also taking on the skies. He was born in Germany in 1874. After leaving Germany as an orphan at about the age of twelve, he had several stints as a sailor. Then Whitehead immigrated to the United States around 1894.

Gustave Whitehead embraced adventure after leaving his home in Germany—including a dream of flying his own plane.

This photo shows a flying machine built by Gustave Whitehead.

He got a job with the Boston Aeronautical Society in 1897. He made a glider for the society, but it was never flown. Whitehead continued building gliders. Some say he was also experimenting with engines. While working at a mine in Pennsylvania, Whitehead started working on a new flying machine.

HE DID WHAT?

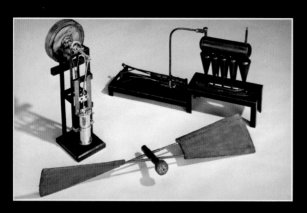

This photo shows a steam engine and a boiler made for a flying machine in the nineteenth century. It gives an idea of how the materials Whitehead was working with might have looked.

To make a light but powerful steam engine, Whitehead experimented at home. He tested **boilers** to see how much pressure he could get. More pressure equaled better flight power. But the tests led to explosions. Some explosions were so loud they broke windows in his neighborhood!

FIRST FLIGHTS?

Whitehead met a man named Louis Darvarich at the mine and told him of his machine. Darvarich described a flight in 1899: "I was present and flew with Mr. Whitehead on the occasion when he succeeded in flying his machine, propelled by steam motor, on a flight of approximately a half mile [0.8 km] distance, at a height of about 20 to 25 feet [6 to 7.6 m] from the ground." The machine hit a building and crashed. Darvarich was the only witness.

Whitehead came back swinging, taking another shot at flight in 1901. This time, he was in Bridgeport, Connecticut. *Scientific American* reported on the craft, which Whitehead called No. 21. It had birdlike wings. On August 14, Whitehead was ready to test it. Richard Howell of the *Bridgeport Herald* had a ringside view. He wrote that the airplane flew half a mile (0.8 km) about 50 feet (15 m) above the ground.

Next, Whitehead built a plane he dubbed No. 22. It had a **kerosene** motor. It may have flown twice in 1902. Whitehead wrote that his plane traveled 2 miles (3.2 km) and made a full turn.

If the writings are true, these flights took place before the Wrights' flights. But Whitehead didn't record details of his experiments. With their proof of flight, the Wrights were declared the winners. Yet Whitehead's claims would resurface about thirty years later. The fight wasn't finished.

CHAPTER 3
THE FIGHT FOR FIRST

After that day at Kill Devil Hills in 1903, the Wrights perfected their plane. They secured a **patent** and shared their flying machine with the world. Soon they were building and selling airplanes. It was well known by then—the Wrights had invented the airplane.

The Wright brothers kept pursuing their dream to pilot planes in the years following their first flight. This plane is being flown by Orville Wright in 1905.

Glenn Curtiss, shown here behind the controls of a plane, got caught up in a patent battle with the Wright brothers.

But not everyone agreed. Whitehead's name was thrown into the ring in 1913. At that time, a lawsuit was brewing against aviator Glenn Curtiss, whom the Wright brothers believed had **infringed** on their patent. As part of their defense, Curtiss's lawyers questioned whether the Wrights were the first to fly. Whitehead and others may have preceded them. The court ruled in the Wrights' favor, but Whitehead's name didn't disappear.

This image shows flight enthusiasts testing a model of Whitehead's aircraft in 1986 to see if its wings were capable of flight.

THE *POPULAR AVIATION* STORY

Although Whitehead died in 1927, his supporters kept his name alive. In 1935 a story was published in *Popular Aviation* magazine. Authors Stella Randolph and Harvey Phillips wrote about Whitehead's flights in the article "Did Whitehead Precede Wright[s] in World's First Powered Flight?" The *Bridgeport Herald* article of 1901 was the inspiration for the story. Randolph wrote a full book about the flights in 1937.

The ball seemed to be back in Whitehead's court. But it irritated Orville Wright, the surviving Wright brother. He threw out a counterpunch, saying that Randolph's claims were unbelievable. After all, Randolph worked in a doctor's office and had little knowledge of aviation. How could her story be trusted?

See Back Cover !

POPULAR AVIATION

JANUARY 25c
In Canada 30c

Bristol Fighters
See Page 40

1935

Popular Aviation brought Whitehead into the spotlight in a very big way.

Scholar John Crane investigated Randolph's claims in 1936. He found that Whitehead's wife and children had never seen him fly. He also found holes in the evidence Randolph cited in her writing. Crane concluded that Whitehead didn't fly before the Wrights, and after that, he may have made short hops in his planes. Whitehead was down for the count.

THE *READER'S DIGEST* ARTICLE

In 1945, a *Reader's Digest* story brought Whitehead back into the ring. It was based on a radio interview with Whitehead's son Charles. Wright once again came back swinging, writing a *U.S. Air Services Magazine* article titled "The Mythical Whitehead Flight."

Wright said the *Bridgeport Herald* story was printed four days after the flight supposedly happened. Why the delay for such an important event? And the story was printed with the headline "Flying," which was illustrated with witches riding brooms. How could that be taken seriously? At the time, "yellow journalism" was common. Newspapers were competitive. False details were sometimes added to make articles more interesting. The *Herald* article also said a man named Andrew Cellie witnessed the flight. Yet another named witness, James Dickie, had never heard of Cellie. To Wright, Whitehead's claims of flight were simply false.

GUSTAVE WHITEHEAD'S STORY.

WHITEHEAD'S FLYING MACHINE SOARING ABOVE THE TREES

CUSTEAD'S AIR SHIP

GUSTAVE WHITEHEAD
(Specially Photographed for the Herald.)

Orville Wright criticized this *Bridgeport Herald* story about Whitehead. The story's headline is illustrated with a group of witches taking flight on brooms.

CHAPTER 4
UNDISPUTED

Although Orville Wright died in 1948, the battle for the first flight title raged on. Some were still convinced Whitehead had flown. Every couple of decades, Whitehead's name came up again.

Stories about Whitehead (*above*) and his flying machines have regularly resurfaced in the news.

Historian John Brown claims that a photo in this Smithsonian exhibit shows Whitehead's 1901 flight.

The most recent claim surfaced in 2013. Flight historian John Brown brought Whitehead back as a contender. While researching at the Smithsonian, he found a photo of a 1906 aviation exhibit with many photos on the wall of the room. Brown says that one of those photos shows Whitehead flying in 1901. Was this a score for Whitehead?

The aviation magazine *Jane's All the World's Aircraft* believed Brown had proof of Whitehead's flight. The publication named Whitehead the first to fly. But the photo didn't convince many others. It had to be enhanced to show

Actor Cliff Robertson raises his arms in triumph after test piloting a replica of Whitehead's plane on July 11, 1986.

what Brown says it shows. The enhancements made the picture blur, and the details are hard to interpret.

The Smithsonian's head **curator** of early flight, Tom Crouch, wasn't convinced. Crouch noted that Whitehead made planes with different designs after his supposed first flight. If his earlier plane worked, why would Whitehead change the design?

ASSIST

Santos-Dumont sits behind his plane's controls in this 1907 photo.

Even if Whitehead wasn't the first to fly, he contributed to aviation by getting others interested in it. Other aviators also assisted in promoting flight. Brazil's Alberto Santos-Dumont was one of them. And many Brazilians believe *he*—not the Wrights or Whitehead—was the first to fly.

Santos-Dumont first flew in 1906. So why do Brazilians claim he beat the Wrights? It's because the Wrights used a launching rail in their first flight. Santos-Dumont did not. This leads some to say that Santos-Dumont flew the first "real" plane.

We may never know if Whitehead flew. But we know the Wrights did. Their photos and data are strong evidence. The Wright brothers' 1903 flight is undisputable.

This photo captures a 1908 flight by Wilbur Wright in France.

THE WINNER!

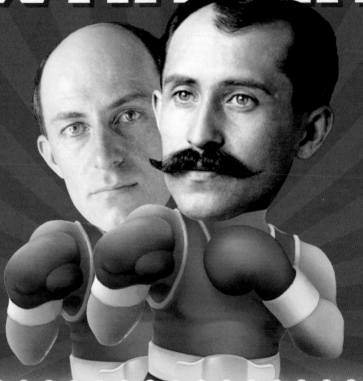

WRIGHT BROTHERS

INVENTOR MATCHUP

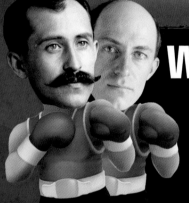

WRIGHT BROTHERS

- **POSITION:** Bicycle mechanics

- **TEAM OR SOLO:** Team

- **A MAJOR ACHIEVEMENT:** Developed wing warping as a way to control flight

- **BIGGEST CLAIM TO FAME:** Flew their plane in 1903, with a photo, data, and witnesses to prove it

VS.

WHITEHEAD

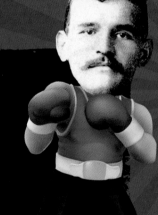

- **POSITION:** Coal miner

- **TEAM OR SOLO:** Solo

- **A MAJOR ACHIEVEMENT:** Built a glider for the Boston Aeronautical Society

- **BIGGEST CLAIM TO FAME:** Stated that he flew in 1899, 1901, and 1902 but has no photos or data to prove it

TIMELINE

1897
Gustave Whitehead builds a glider for the Boston Aeronautical Society, but it never flies.

1899
Louis Darvarich says that he helped Whitehead fly a steam-powered flying machine. The Wrights invent wing warping, a key to controlled flight.

1900
The Wright brothers begin testing gliders at Kitty Hawk and Kill Devil Hills, North Carolina.

1901
Whitehead flies No. 21, and the story is reported in the *Bridgeport Herald*.

1902
Whitehead flies No. 22, making a turn in the sky.

1903
On December 17, the Wrights make what most US historians consider the first official controlled and powered flight.

1935
A *Popular Aviation* story claims that Whitehead flew before the Wright brothers.

2013
John Brown claims he found proof of Whitehead's first flight in a photograph, but the Smithsonian denies that claim.

SOURCE NOTES

10 Stephen Kirk, *First in Flight: The Wright Brothers in North Carolina* (Winston-Salem, NC: John F. Blair, 1995), 82.

14 Martin W. Sandler, *Lost to Time: Unforgettable Stories That History Forgot* (New York: Sterling, 2010), 209.

GLOSSARY

boilers: tanks that heat water to make steam, which can be used to power a motor

curator: the person in charge of a museum or gallery

gliders: light aircraft that fly without the power of a motor

gyroscopes: tools that have a wheel that spins inside a frame to balance in any position

infringed: failed to obey or act in agreement with a law or a patent

kerosene: a thin, colorless fuel made from petroleum

lift: the force that holds an airplane in the air, made by an airplane's motion

patent: a legal document giving an inventor of something the only rights to make or sell that invention

propellers: sets of rotating blades that provide force to move an airplane through the air

rudders: hinged plates on an airplane that are used for steering

FURTHER READING

Buckley, James, Jr. *Who Were the Wright Brothers?* New York: Grosset & Dunlap, 2014.

Farndon, John. *Stickmen's Guide to Aircraft.* Minneapolis: Hungry Tomato, 2016.

Hutchison, Patricia. *The Invention of the Airplane.* Mankato, MN: Child's World, 2017.

NASA: History of Flight
https://www.grc.nasa.gov/www/k-12/UEET/StudentSite
/historyofflight.html

Schulz, Walter A. *Johnny Moore and the Wright Brothers' Flying Machine.* Minneapolis: Millbrook Press, 2011.

Smithsonian: "How Do Things Fly?"
http://howthingsfly.si.edu

INDEX

PHOTO ACKNOWLEDGEMENTS

The images in this book are used with the permission of: iStock.com/eduardrobert, p. 1; iStock.com/dell640, p. 4; © Dorling Kindersley/Thinkstock, pp. 5, 9; iStock.com/triggermouse, p. 6; Library of Congress, pp. 7 (both), 10, 11, 16, 17, 22, 27, 28 (Wrights); © Laura Westlund/Independent Picture Service, p. 8; ullstein bild akg images/Newscom (Whitehead), pp. 12, 28; Smithsonian National Air and Space Museum, p. 13 (NASM-SI-81-16184), p. 23 (NASM-SI-2009-4596-A); Science & Society Picture Library/Getty Images, p. 14; Aviation History Collection/Alamy Stock Photo, p. 18; Popular Aviation, January 1935, p. 19; Bridgeport Herald August 18 1901, p. 21; AP Photo/Peter Hvizdak, p. 24; Bettmann/Getty Images, p. 25; Philipp Kester/ullstein bild/Getty Images, p. 26. Design elements: iStock.com/ivanastar; iStock.com/Allevinatis; iStock.com/subtropica; iStock.com/lushik.

Cover: Library of Congress (Wrights); ullstein bild akg images/Newscom (Whitehead); iStock.com/eduardrobert (propeller).